DISCOVERING

THE
U.S.A.

By Cass R. Sandak

A ZOË BOOK

A ZOË BOOK

© 1994 Zoë Books Limited

Devised and produced by
Zoë Books Limited
15 Worthy Lane
Winchester
Hampshire SO23 7AB
England

First published in Great Britain in 1994 by
Zoë Books Limited
15 Worthy Lane
Winchester
Hampshire SO23 7AB

Reprinted in 1994

A record of the CIP data is available from the British Library.

ISBN 1 874488 25 8

Printed in Italy by Grafedit SpA
Design: Jan Sterling, Sterling Associates
Picture research: Victoria Sturgess
Map: Gecko Limited
Production: Grahame Griffiths

Photographic acknowledgments

The publishers wish to acknowledge, with thanks, the following photographic sources:

Cover: Zefa; title page: Impact Photos / Michael George; 5l & r, 6, Robert Harding Picture Library; 7l Frank Sloan; 7r, 8, 9l & r Robert Harding Picture Library; 10 Impact Photos / Alain le Garsmeur; 11l Frank Sloan; 11r Robert Harding Picture Library; 12 Zefa; 13l & r Robert Harding Picture Library; 14 Impact Photos / Alastair Indge; 15l Frank Sloan; 15r The Hutchison Library / Liba Taylor; 16 Wayne Schwaeber; 17l Zefa; 17r Karen Pandell; 18, 19l Zefa; 19r The Hutchison Library / Liba Taylor; 20, 21l Robert Harding Picture Library; 21r Zefa; 22 Allsport / Rick Stewart; 23l The Hutchison Library / Robert Francis; 23r, 24 Robert Harding Picture Library; 25l & r Frank Sloan; 26 Robert Harding Picture Library; 27l National Gallery, Washington D.C.; 27r Hulton Deutsch Collection / The Bettmann Archive; 28 Hulton Deutsch Collection; 29l Peter Newark's Western Americana; 29r NASA

Cover: *The White House, Washington, D.C.*

Title page: *A tickertape parade on New York's Broadway*

Contents

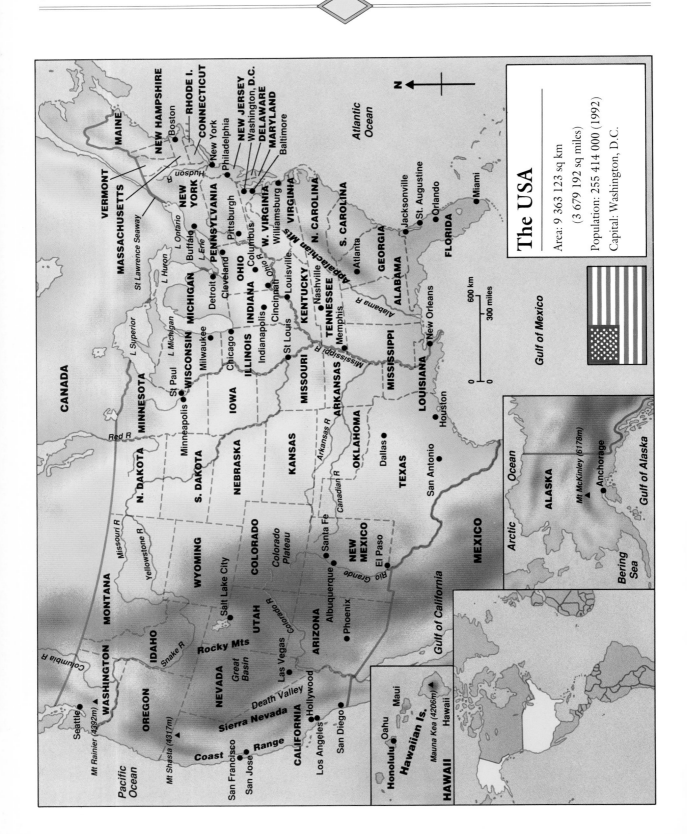

The USA

Area: 9 363 123 sq km
(3 679 192 sq miles)
Population: 255 414 000 (1992)
Capital: Washington, D.C.

600 km
300 miles

N

CANADA

MEXICO

Atlantic Ocean

Pacific Ocean

Gulf of Mexico

Gulf of California

WASHINGTON
Seattle •
Mt Rainier (4392m) ▲
OREGON
IDAHO
MONTANA
Columbia R
Snake R
Mt Shasta (4317m) ▲
Coast Range
Sierra Nevada
NEVADA
Great Basin
Death Valley
San Francisco •
San Jose •
Hollywood •
Los Angeles •
San Diego •
CALIFORNIA
Las Vegas •
UTAH
Salt Lake City •
WYOMING
Yellowstone R
Missouri R
Rocky Mts
ARIZONA
Phoenix •
COLORADO
Colorado Plateau
Colorado R
Santa Fe •
Albuquerque •
NEW MEXICO
El Paso •
Rio Grande
N. DAKOTA
S. DAKOTA
NEBRASKA
KANSAS
OKLAHOMA
TEXAS
Dallas •
San Antonio •
Houston •
Red R
Arkansas R
Canadian R
MINNESOTA
St Paul •
Minneapolis •
IOWA
MISSOURI
St Louis •
ARKANSAS
LOUISIANA
New Orleans •
WISCONSIN
Milwaukee •
ILLINOIS
Chicago •
Indianapolis •
INDIANA
MISSISSIPPI
Memphis •
TENNESSEE
Nashville •
ALABAMA
MICHIGAN
Detroit •
OHIO
Cleveland •
Columbus •
Cincinnati •
KENTUCKY
Louisville •
Ohio R
Mississippi R
Alabama R
Atlanta •
GEORGIA
FLORIDA
Orlando •
Jacksonville •
St. Augustine •
Miami •
L Superior
L Michigan
L Huron
L Ontario
L Erie
Buffalo •
PENNSYLVANIA
Pittsburgh •
St Lawrence Seaway
Hudson R
VERMONT
NEW HAMPSHIRE
MAINE
MASSACHUSETTS
Boston •
RHODE I.
CONNECTICUT
NEW YORK
New York •
Philadelphia •
NEW JERSEY
Washington, D.C.
DELAWARE
MARYLAND
Baltimore •
W. VIRGINIA
VIRGINIA
Williamsburg •
N. CAROLINA
S. CAROLINA
Appalachian Mts

Arctic Ocean
Bering Sea
Gulf of Alaska
ALASKA
Mt McKinley (6178m) ▲
Anchorage •

HAWAII
Hawaiian Is.
Oahu
Honolulu •
Maui
Mauna Kea (4206m) ▲
Hawaii

Welcome to the USA!

The United States of America (USA) stretch across the North American continent from the Canadian border southwards to Mexico and range almost 4800 km from east to west. The country is made up of 48 states which border one another. There are also two other states, Alaska and Hawaii. Alaska lies beyond Canadian territory and extends northwards to the Arctic Ocean. The islands of Hawaii lie far to the west, in the Pacific Ocean.

This vast country includes deserts and swamps, open grasslands or prairies, snowy mountains, and great forests. There may even be different climates and terrains within one state.

The USA still has many remote rural areas, but most people live and work in urban areas or in the many large cities. These cities are linked by networks of rail, road and air routes.

A truck on a lonely highway

Native Americans in New Mexico

The people

People in the USA are as varied as the land itself. The Native Americans were the first to settle on the continent, around 50 000 years ago. These first inhabitants originally came from Asia and included peoples later called American Indians.

European settlers, from Spain, France, the Netherlands and the British Isles, arrived in the south and east of North America during the 1500s and 1600s. There were also Africans, brought to work as slaves. Later more settlers came from all over the world.

As a result, the people of the USA today are a mix of many races, religions and nationalities. Many people follow the traditions and cultures of their ethnic background, but most people see themselves firstly as US citizens.

Around the Northeast

The six states of Maine, New Hampshire, Vermont, Massachusetts, Connecticut and Rhode Island make up the region known as New England. This area has played a very important part in the history of the USA.

New England takes its name from the first European settlers in the area. Some of these were English Christians called 'Pilgrims', a group of Puritans who wanted freedom to worship in their own way. They were not allowed to do so in England. The Pilgrims first landed in Plymouth, Massachusetts, in 1620. Puritans then founded the Massachusetts Bay Colony in 1628.

Boston became the first large town in New England and played an important part in the colonists' struggle for independence from Britain in the 1770s. Today Boston is an industrial city with a population of more than half a million. The neighbouring town, Cambridge, is the site of the first college in the USA, Harvard University.

New England is a beautiful region, with low mountains and trees that turn red, brown and gold in the autumn. It has a rugged, rocky coast on the stormy Atlantic Ocean. Cape Cod, a great hook-shaped spit of land, is named after the plentiful fish in the sea around it.

New York, New York

While the English were settling New England, most of the Hudson River

The Stars and Stripes *flies outside this timber-built house in Vermont.*

Valley was being colonized by the Dutch. Later the area came under British rule.

New York state has long been an important centre of influence in the USA. Its large port, New York City, is protected from the Atlantic Ocean by a vast natural harbour. The city has been the gateway for millions of immigrants.

Today New York City has a population of over 7 million and is the country's largest city. At its centre is the island of Manhattan, whose skyline is a forest of tall, gleaming buildings. They include some of the world's most famous skyscrapers, such as the Empire State Building and the World Trade Centre.

New York City is an international centre of industry and commerce. The US business world is based around Wall Street. Theatres line the famous street called Broadway. New York attracts lovers of dance, ballet, opera, music and art from all over the world.

The Statue of Liberty

The Empire State Building, Manhattan

Ellis Island – and Liberty

From 1892 until 1943 tiny Ellis Island, in New York's harbour, was the immigration centre for most foreigners arriving in the USA. It was the first view of North America for some 17 million people.

Nearby on Liberty Island is the Statue of Liberty. This gift from the people of France is a world-famous symbol of freedom.

Mid-Atlantic states

The states of New Jersey, Delaware and Pennsylvania lie on the Atlantic Coast. Pennsylvania, whose chief city is Philadelphia, was founded by Quakers. Settlers later moved west and discovered the coal, iron and oil that brought wealth to the new country. The steel industry made Pittsburgh, in western Pennsylvania, a great industrial city.

The capital city

The Capitol, Washington, D.C.

The District of Columbia (D.C.) is not a state or a part of one. Its territory was created from 179 square kilometres of Virginia and Maryland. Washington, D.C., is the capital of the USA and the centre of US government.

The city is named after George Washington (1732-99), the first president of the USA. He lived nearby at Mount Vernon, Virginia, and thought this once swampy site on the banks of the Potomac River would make a good place for the nation's capital. Every US president after George Washington has lived in the city during his term of office.

Washington, D.C., was laid out by a French architect called Pierre L'Enfant. The city has broad, open streets and avenues. Above them rises the gleaming white dome of the Capitol, the meeting place of the US Congress.

The official home of the president and his family is the White House. Most of this fine mansion was built in the 1790s and was first occupied by President John Adams and his wife, Abigail. It is said she hung the washing in the unfinished East Room, now the scene of formal occasions!

Washington is a city of grand public buildings, spacious parks and gardens, fountains and pools. In spring the blossom from thousands of Japanese cherry trees along the Potomac fills the city with beauty and fragrance. Many government officials live in Georgetown, a fashionable part of the city with elegant homes and stately mansions. A number of these buildings are about 200 years old.

Politics and presidents

The United States is a democracy, in which the people vote for those who represent them. The two biggest political parties in the USA are the Republicans and the Democrats.

There are three branches of government. The first is Congress, which makes the laws. Congress consists of the Senate and the House of Representatives. The second is the Supreme Court. The nine justices of the Court interpret the law. The third branch, the Executive, enforces the law and governs the country. It includes the president, the vice-president and members of the Cabinet.

A street in Georgetown

The Memorial Statue of Abraham Lincoln

Sights to see

Washington Monument – One of the city's best-known landmarks, this tall obelisk, or column, was finished in 1884 and dedicated the next year.

Smithsonian Institution – Begun in 1846, this group of museums is sometimes called 'the nation's attic'.

Lincoln Memorial – Dedicated in 1922, this great building contains a famous statue of Abraham Lincoln (1809-65), the 16th president.

Arlington National Cemetery – In nearby Virginia, this is the final resting place for many US military figures, as well as President John F. Kennedy who was killed in 1963.

National Gallery – The east and west wings house one of the world's greatest collections of paintings.

The Library of Congress – This fine building contains copies of every book published in the USA.

Zoo and Botanical Garden – Both preserve rare species of animals and plants for study and enjoyment.

The South

The southeastern states lie between the Atlantic Ocean and the Gulf of Mexico. They include Virginia, West Virginia, Maryland, Kentucky, Tennessee, North and South Carolina, Georgia, Florida, Alabama and Mississippi. They are often referred to simply as the South.

Many of the southern states tried to break away from the USA in the 1860s, an event that led to the American Civil War. One reason for this war was a bitter dispute over slavery. At that time 4 million African Americans worked as slaves on southern plantations – large farms that exported tobacco and cotton to the rest of the world. While the white plantation owners enjoyed a gracious and

Horses racing in the Kentucky Derby

relaxed way of life, most of the slaves lived in very poor conditions.

The first permanent English settlement in Virginia was founded in 1607 at Jamestown. Many tourists visit Williamsburg, Virginia, where buildings of the colonial period have been restored. Virginia's western border is formed by the Appalachians, a mountain chain that stretches southwards through the eastern states.

Many fine racehorses are raised in Kentucky, the Bluegrass state, and a famous horse race, the Kentucky Derby, is held in Louisville each spring. Kentucky

The city centre skyline in Atlanta

is also the site of the Mammoth Caves, one of the world's largest underground cave systems. Some 500 kilometres of these caves have been mapped.

Tennessee is the home of two kinds of popular music. Nashville is the site of the Grand Ole Opry, a theatre which is known as the home of country-and-western music. At Memphis, fans of rock-and-roll visit Graceland, the lavish home built by Elvis Presley, star of the 1950s and 60s.

Southern attractions

The southernmost states enjoy fairly warm and humid weather much of the year. The climate has attracted both permanent residents and tourists to the area. Modern businesses, such as the computer industry, have also been attracted to southern cities in recent years.

At Kitty Hawk, North Carolina, Orville and Wilbur Wright flew the first powered aeroplane in 1903. Further south is the charming city of Charleston, South Carolina. Much of the city remains just as it was more than 100 years ago. In contrast, Atlanta, Georgia, is one of the country's fastest-growing cities. Atlanta's Hartsfield Airport is one of the largest and the third busiest in the USA.

The oldest city in the USA is St. Augustine, Florida. It was founded in 1565 by the Spanish. Florida's attractions include Daytona Beach, where cars are raced on the sand, and Cape Canaveral, launching site for US space flights. People of all ages visit Orlando to see Disney World, the internationally famous theme park. Many people settle in Florida after they retire from work.

Wildlife at large

Florida's Everglades form a vast wetland area which is a safe haven for alligators, poisonous snakes and rare birds. There are 51 National Parks, 155 National Forests, and almost 500 National Wildlife Refuges in the USA.

An alligator in the Everglades

West of the Mississippi

During the 1600s and 1700s the French and Spanish explored the valleys of the Mississippi and Missouri rivers. In 1803 the French sold a vast corridor of land, stretching from north to south, to the USA. It was called the Louisiana Purchase. Today's state of Louisiana covers only a small part of the original territory.

The states of Louisiana, Arkansas, Missouri, Kansas, Oklahoma, Texas, New Mexico and Colorado may be grouped together as the south-central states.

French influence can still be seen in New Orleans, the Louisiana city built on the steamy delta where the Mississippi meets the Gulf of Mexico. The old centre of the city, with its wrought iron balconies and small courtyards, is known as the French Quarter. Each year just before Lent a famous parade and a series of fancy dress balls are held to celebrate *Mardi Gras.* New Orleans is the home of jazz.

Hot springs in what is now Arkansas were first found to be good for the health by the Native American peoples living in the region long ago. The springs were used by Spanish explorers in the 1500s and are still popular today. To the west lie the grasslands and farms of Kansas and Oklahoma.

A jazz band playing in the French Quarter, New Orleans

Rounding up cattle in New Mexico

The mighty river

The Mississippi river rises in Minnesota and flows southwards, joined on the way by two other great rivers, the Ohio and the Missouri. Together they form the biggest river system in the USA, 3745 kilometres long. Before reaching the coast of the Gulf of Mexico, the Mississippi divides into a maze of waterways, forming a delta.

Remember the Alamo!

San Antonio is the site of the Alamo, a mission where a handful of Texans fought bravely against an army of Spaniards in 1836. One of the fighters was Davy Crockett, made famous by song and legend. At that time Texas was part of Mexico and ruled by Spain. The modern border with Mexico runs along the Rio Grande.

Plains and mountains

Texas is the second largest state in the USA – a vast, dry plain dotted with cactus and tumbleweed. The state grew rich on cattle and oil in the 19th century. It is still a land of ranches and oil wells, but Texas is now also one of the most modern states in the USA. Three of the ten largest cities in the USA are in Texas. They are Houston, Dallas, and San Antonio, a centre of industry – including cowboy boot manufacture.

To the west lies New Mexico. Here too the Spanish colonial influence can still be seen in the cities of Albuquerque and Santa Fé. The landscape includes limestone rock which, over the ages, has been worn away by underground streams. The famous Carlsbad Caverns are home for countless bats.

Colorado is crossed by some of the most rugged of the Rocky Mountains, which extend northwards across the continent. Pikes Peak (4301 metres) became a famous landmark in the 1850s, when mining prospectors were hurrying west in search of gold. Today's visitors enjoy the skiing slopes and the hiking trails.

On the ski lift, Breckenridge, Colorado

Lakes and prairies

The north-central states include Ohio, Indiana, Illinois, Michigan, Wisconsin, Iowa, Minnesota, Nebraska, and North and South Dakota. The weather here is generally mild and warm in the summer, but the winters can be bitterly cold.

This is the land of the Great Lakes. There are five Great Lakes in all – Erie, Ontario, Huron, Michigan and Superior. Together they cover 246 050 square kilometres and form the largest body of fresh water in the world.

The Great Lakes were the main route for transporting goods inland from the Atlantic coast in the early

A view of the Detroit waterfront

days of the European settlers. Goods were also carried long distances across New York state until the Erie Canal was opened. Today the St. Lawrence Seaway, along the Canadian border, connects the Great Lakes with the Atlantic Ocean.

On four wheels

Detroit, Michigan, the home of US car or automobile manufacture, has been nicknamed 'Motown'. The pioneer of the car industry Henry Ford (1863-1947) was born at Dearborn,

The Sears Tower, Chicago

near Detroit. In the 1930s Ford reconstructed the historic Greenfield Village, including the workplaces of distinguished US inventors.

To the south, Indianapolis, the state capital of Indiana, is the site of the world-famous Speedway. The '500' motor race is held there each May.

Sky high

The world's tallest building is the Sears Tower in Chicago, Illinois. It is 443 metres high and has 110 storeys. It was finished in 1973. Some of the world's first skyscrapers were built in Chicago, after a fire destroyed much of the city in 1871.

Chicago

For many years Chicago, Illinois, was known as the 'Second City', but today, with a population of over 2.7 million, it is only the third largest city in the USA, after New York City and Los Angeles. However, the city is thriving, with a lively area along the lakeshore and a smart city centre. Part of this area is called 'The Loop', after the raised section of the local railway system which circles it.

Into the country

The rural Midwest is a vast area. Ohio has forests replanted over areas destroyed by the industry of the 19th century. To the west the land has gently rolling grasslands, or prairies. Iowa and other farm states are known as the 'Corn Belt' because of the large grain harvests they produce. Wisconsin is noted for dairy farming. Minnesota claims to have no fewer than 15 000 lakes. South Dakota is famous for its Black Hills. There, between 1927 and 1941, Mount Rushmore was carved with the faces of four US presidents.

Cornfields and a farmhouse in Iowa

The Wild West

The Rocky Mountains divide the continent and form the watershed. To the east, rivers drain into the Gulf of Mexico. To the west, they drain into the Pacific Ocean.

The far west of the USA lies beyond the mountain states of Idaho, Montana and Wyoming. Yellowstone, the country's oldest National Park, lies across the borders where these three states meet. It is famous for its grizzly bears and its 10 000 geysers, or natural springs.

To the south and west are three desert states, Utah, Nevada and Arizona. Utah is a land of canyons and ancient rocks, worn into strange pillars and arches. Dazzling, white salt deserts form a vast, empty expanse of land. Salt Lake City was founded in 1847 by the Mormons.

In Las Vegas, Nevada, neon lights which advertise casinos and shows rise above the desert sands. The city is a centre for gambling and entertainment.

The Colorado River flows through deep channels in the desert rock. The most spectacular of these is Arizona's Grand Canyon, the world's deepest land gorge. It is 443 kilometres long and averages 1.5 kilometres in depth.

The shimmering, hot deserts of the southwest are home to American Indian peoples such as the Navajo. Here, too, is Phoenix, Arizona, one of the fastest-growing cities in the country.

A helicopter ride is one of the best ways to see the Grand Canyon.

Surfers in California

The West Coast

Mountain ranges run parallel to the North Pacific coast. Major peaks include Mount Rainier (4392 metres) and Mount St Helens, a volcano that erupted in 1980. The domes, peaks and waterfalls of Yosemite Valley are among the most beautiful sights in the USA.

The main port on the northwest coast is Seattle. The states of Washington and Oregon have cool, rainy weather and forests green with moss and ferns.

The state of California stretches down the west coast to the Mexican border. Coastal areas enjoy a mild climate, fresh and cool in the north. Coast redwoods and giant sequoias, the largest trees on earth, grow here. It is very warm in the south, so grapevines, fruit, and vegetable crops grow well. Southern parts of the state include deserts such as Death Valley, the lowest point in the country.

Los Angeles, with 3.5 million inhabitants, is a sprawling city linked by motorways and full of traffic. Its rundown urban areas contrast with its attractive, wealthy suburbs. The most famous suburb may be Hollywood, the world centre of the film industry.

To the north lies San Francisco, a city built on steep hills looking over the harbour and Bay. In the 20th century it has been the site of two major earthquakes.

Ice and fire

The most isolated states of the USA are among the most fascinating. Alaska is the largest state of all, a remote wilderness of forests, mountains and glaciers. The highest peak in North America is Mount McKinley (6194 metres). Native Americans of the region include the Aleuts and the Inuit, or Eskimo, peoples.

Hawaii is a Pacific island paradise. Its islands are in fact the peaks of partly submerged volcanoes. Some are still active, sometimes erupting with streams of lava.

Mendenhall Glacier, Alaska

Everyday life

Few workers are needed on this car assembly line in Detroit.

Most men and women work an eight-hour day in the USA. Many live some distance away from their jobs and travel to work by car. About 70 per cent of women with children go out to work. Most people in the USA have shorter holidays than Europeans. They also spend more time travelling on business and have less time to relax at home.

Only about 2 per cent of the workforce is now employed in farming. Jobs in manufacturing are also becoming scarce. This is partly the result of automation, as machines take over the jobs once done by hand. Financial and service industries employ the most workers. Areas of new technology, such as computers and electronics, have created more job opportunities. Careers in law, medicine and education attract many young people.

Many people are wealthy and the 'American dream' – to own a home and at least one car – is still within the reach of many workers. However, the USA, like many other countries, has faced economic problems in recent years. Visitors are often surprised by the amount of poverty still to be seen on the streets of many cities in the USA.

Children pledge loyalty to their country

Housing and homes

Most families live in detached houses. However, more and more young single people, childless couples and elderly people live in flats. Most of these are rented. It is only in the larger cities that whole families live in flats rather than houses.

Religious freedom

The USA has no official religion. Freedom of worship is guaranteed by the Constitution, the basic laws of the country. Over 60 per cent of people in the USA are Christian. These include about 60 million Roman Catholics and 100 million Protestants and other Christians. Their major religious holidays are Christmas and Easter. About 6 million people are Jewish and another 6 million follow Islam. Smaller numbers follow Buddhism, Hinduism and other religions.

Going to school

Throughout the USA there is free state education. There are also many private and religious schools. The school year generally runs from September to June. The school day starts at about 8am and ends at about 3pm, five days a week. After school there are sports and social activities.

Most children start school at the age of 5 or 6. They have to go to school until they are at least 16. There are 12 school grades. Grades 9 or 10 up to 12 are known as 'high school'. High school leavers may start work or go on to college.

Health care

The USA has a private health care system. This means that most people must pay insurance to receive medical treatment. In 1993, President Bill Clinton, proposed reforming the system to include millions of people who had no insurance.

Jewish children reading the Torah

Food in the USA

Many people stop at a café for a quick breakfast on the way to work. They may have fruit juice, coffee or tea, with a doughnut, muffin, Danish pastry or a bagel. A family breakfast at home is usually larger. The meal could include ham, sausage or bacon with eggs, pancakes or waffles with maple syrup.

Business people tend to eat large lunches, often at expensive restaurants. Even so, many of these restaurants now offer salads and light meals, so people can eat more healthily. Other people eat cheaper, smaller lunches such as salads, a slice of pizza or sandwiches. Some people eat at fast-food restaurants, which serve hamburgers, hot dogs, chips, and milk shakes or ice-cream sodas.

The evening meal is usually a large one, whether it is eaten at home or in a restaurant. A great deal of food in the USA comes, like the population, from foreign sources. Chinese, French and Italian dishes are very popular.

Because so many men and women work long hours away from home, convenience foods are more popular than ever. In cities, supermarkets and corner shops may be open 24 hours a day. In some places smaller food shops have been forced out of business. However, there are still bakers, butchers, and open-air markets selling fresh fruit and vegetables in many places.

The quickest way to get a take-away meal is to use a fast food 'drive-in'.

Regional specialities

Many regions in the USA produce their own special food and drinks. Many of these have now become popular all over the country.

- New England is famous for its creamy soup – clam chowder, lobsters, and a dessert called Indian pudding. Boston is the home of baked beans.
- Maryland is known for its oysters and crabs, from Chesapeake Bay.
- Kentucky is famous for its fried chicken.
- Texas is proud of its local beef. Large, juicy steaks are cooked at barbecues. 'Tex-Mex' is a blend of southwestern and true Mexican cooking.
- Louisiana is the home of Cajun cooking. Popular dishes include spicy shrimps and gumbo, a tasty vegetable soup or stew.
- California is known around the world for its wines.
- Hawaii offers a Polynesian feast called a *luau*. It includes a roasted suckling pig, complete with head, served with fish heads, rice and pineapples.

Preparing food for a street party

A famous southern dish – soft-shell crab

Thanksgiving dinner

The fourth Thursday in November is a traditional holiday. It was first celebrated by the settlers in New England who wanted to give thanks for having survived their first year in North America. The food for the Thanksgiving dinner was the same then as it is today – roast turkey, cranberry sauce and pumpkin pie.

Fast food

People in the USA like their food tasty, cheap – and quick. Chains of fast-food restaurants, serving hamburgers or chicken, first grew up in the USA and are now seen in cities around the world. The food is not always very nutritious, so now some chains are producing healthier food.

All sorts of sport

Spectator sports have a wide following in the USA. College and university sports, especially American football, are very popular, but the professional teams attract the largest crowds. Many large cities in the USA sponsor their own teams for baseball, American football, basketball and ice hockey. There are great rivalries between the major teams and their loyal fans.

There are two special dates on the sporting calendar. The Super Bowl is a match between the winners of the two main American football divisions. It is

The Dallas Cowboys beat the Buffalo Bills at the Super Bowl, in January 1993.

Volleyball in Central Park, New York City

held each year on a Sunday in January. The World Series is a group of baseball games between winning teams from the National League and the American League. It is held in October. Millions of people watch these events on television.

Keeping fit

People don't just watch sport, they enjoy taking part – whether in competition or just for fun. Amateur games of baseball, softball and basketball are played in parks and on courts in many towns. Tennis, squash and golf are also popular. Many people keep fit by jogging, running or doing aerobic exercises in time to music.

The great outdoors

At the weekend, or during the summer holidays, people love to head for the countryside or the coast. They may drive to a camp site in a National Park, forest or recreational area. Some families own 'RVs' (Recreational Vehicles), which have electricity, running water and cookers.

People stay near lakes or coasts because swimming, boating, fishing and water-skiing are all popular sports. Wherever there is a fast-moving river, especially in the canyons of the western states, people can go white-water rafting or canoeing. The rolling ocean waves of California and Hawaii are the best for surfers.

Rock climbers go to the peaks of Colorado, or to California's Yosemite Valley, to practise their skills.

On the trail

There are hiking paths and trails in almost every part of the country. Some trails cross very remote areas of forest or mountains. Many people use the trails for backpacking, horse-riding or cross-country skiing.

Backpacking in Wyoming

Arts and leisure

The mixture of different peoples in the USA has led to an exciting variety of artistic expression. This is particularly true of popular music and dance in the USA, both of which have been influenced by the cultures of western Africa, the British Isles, France, Spain and other areas. The results have travelled around the world – jazz, country-and-western, soul music, blues, rock music, folk and rap.

The shows and entertainment of the 1800s led to the lively musicals in the 20th century. The energy of the new country was also expressed in classical music, ballet and modern dance, and opera. Many cities have famous orchestras, dance and opera companies.

Filming on a set for a 'western'

As well as collecting tapes and CDs, young people are interested in videos and television. Cable television networks make it possible for viewers to receive many different TV channels, even in remote areas.

During the 20th century, it was cinema and television that showed life in the USA to the rest of the world. Hollywood is still the centre of the film industry, and its Academy Awards – the Oscars – are eagerly awaited each year.

Art and architecture

The traditional art of the Native Americans included beautiful jewellery, carvings and pottery. Early settlers were also skilled in crafts and made fine furniture and needlework. Painters recorded the landscape and the wildlife they discovered as they travelled west.

The skyscrapers of Chicago, New York and other cities are representative of modern architecture. Some talented artists escaped from wars in Europe and settled in the USA. During the 1950s

An Alexander Calder mobile sculpture

Browsing at a bookstall in New York City

and 60s New York City became the world centre of experimental art. Today some of the world's great art collections are to be found in museums and galleries across the USA.

The written and spoken word

Some people are great readers but many prefer to spend their leisure time in other ways! Both school and libraries provide free access to popular books as well as works of reference. The USA has a large publishing industry.

Writers from the USA have created a rich literature that reflects the country's varied population. Works include short stories, poetry, novels and plays. Some of these plays are performed all over the world.

Many of the best writers in the USA have worked as journalists. Daily papers are published in all the large cities, including the *New York Times*, *Wall Street Journal*, *Los Angeles Times*, *Washington Post* and *Chicago Tribune*.

A long time ago

How did the first people reach North America? Between 60 000 and 10 000 BC the climate changed many times. There were long Ice Ages, with milder periods in between. At times the sea level dropped, and it became possible for hunters from the Siberian region of Asia to cross into North America over a bridge of land.

Over many thousands of years these hunters spread through North America and into Central and South America, where great civilizations developed. In parts of North America they learned to farm, growing maize and beans. Many different ways of life grew up – in the wooded valleys of the East, in the desert canyons of the Southwest, in the fishing villages of the Northwest, and along the Pacific coast.

The first Europeans to land in North America were probably the Vikings, about a thousand years ago. The Spanish reached Florida in 1513, and soon the French were exploring the Great Lakes and following the Mississippi southwards. Settlers also came from the Netherlands, Sweden and Germany. However it was the English who founded the 13 colonies along the east coast which later became the original USA.

The Cliff Palace in Mesa Verde, Colorado, was built more than 1000 years ago.

George Washington

Wars with Britain

The eastern colonists had a number of disputes with the British government over taxes and laws. In 1776 a group of colonists signed the Declaration of Independence, cutting all ties with Great Britain. The War of Independence (or American Revolution) lasted until 1781, when the British surrendered to General George Washington at Yorktown, Virginia.

The Constitution, written in 1787, guaranteed human rights and provided a framework for the US government. Washington was named first president in 1789. Britain was again defeated by the USA in the War of 1812.

Settlers and explorers

In the 19th century many settlers travelled westwards. Some, like Meriwether Lewis and William Clark, explored more remote parts of North America. These two former soldiers used a Native American woman, Sacagawea, as their guide. They crossed the Rocky Mountains and reached the Pacific Coast.

A growing country

The new country grew rapidly. The Louisiana Purchase took place in 1803, and Texas was taken over in 1845. California, New Mexico and other huge tracts of land were gained through the Mexican War of 1846-48.

A railway was built across the continent. Forests were felled and many factories were built. Miners moved to Colorado and California. Farmers and ranchers settled on the prairies, lands used for hunting buffalo by the Native American peoples. A series of Indian wars lasted until 1890. By that time most of the Native American peoples had been forced to move onto reservations.

The American Civil War (1861-65) was a bitter conflict between the northern states of the Union and the southern, or Confederate, states. The leadership of President Abraham Lincoln meant victory for the Union forces and ensured the end of slavery for African Americans.

A regiment of Union foot soldiers

The new country

Film star, Bob Hope, in England to entertain US troops during the Second World War

In the later years of the 19th century, industry grew rapidly in the USA, especially in the Northeast. A few people made a fortune from industries such as steel manufacture and the railways. The USA was turning into one of the world's largest industrial countries. The expanding economy also attracted new waves of immigration – this time from Italy, central and eastern Europe, and China. Many of the newcomers had to work for low wages in poor conditions.

The USA was already a world power when it entered the First World War in 1917. It fought, with France and Great Britain, on the side of the Allies. The USA helped defeat Germany and was involved in the settlements and treaty that ended the terrible war in 1918.

The 1920s saw the vast distances across the USA shrunk – by trains, cars and air travel. It was the age of jazz and the cinema. However, disaster struck when the economy collapsed in 1929. During the Great Depression, which lasted more than ten years, large numbers of workers in the USA faced severe hardship from unemployment.

New York, 1931 – a queue for cheap food

War and peace

In 1941 the USA joined the Second World War, after Japan bombed the US Pacific naval base of Pearl Harbor in Hawaii. The war ended in 1945, after scientists developed nuclear weapons. The US Airforce dropped atomic bombs on two Japanese cities, Hiroshima and Nagasaki.

The Soviet Union, the country now replaced by Russia and other members of the Commonwealth of Independent States, had been an ally of the USA during the Second World War. However, during the 1950s and 60s, the Soviet Union became the main enemy of the USA, which opposed its Communist ideals. Outright war with the Soviet Union was avoided – instead there was a 'cold war'. US troops did fight a long and unsuccessful war against the communists in North Vietnam.

Tragically, some of the most important public figures of the 1960s were gunned down by assassins, including President John F. Kennedy (1917–63) and Dr. Martin Luther King, Jr. (1929–68), who led the long peaceful struggle for black civil rights.

Today people in the USA face many problems, from street riots and violent crime to homelessness and a weakening economy. However the country is rich in resources and people still have the energy and determination to face the challenges of the future.

A US astronaut on the moon, 1973

Fact file

Stars and Stripes

The US flag is sometimes known as the Stars and Stripes or as 'Old Glory'. It has always had 13 stripes, 7 red ones and 6 white.

The stars represent states, and their arrangement has varied over the years as the number of states has grown. At first the blue canton, or box, contained a circle of 13 white stars. Now there are 50 stars arranged in 5 rows of six stars and 4 rows of five stars.

National anthem

The anthem is called *The Star-Spangled Banner*. It was written by Francis Scott Key during a battle in the War of 1812, near Baltimore, Maryland. It became the official anthem in 1931.

The national emblem

This includes the bald eagle – a large, fish-eating bird of prey which has become endangered in recent years. It is still found in large numbers in Alaska and has returned to some other states.

Money matters

One dollar ($1) is made up of 100 cents. One cent is called a penny. Five cents is called a nickel and 10 cents a dime. 25 cents is called a quarter, and the 50 cent coin a half-dollar. The smaller bank notes ($1, $5, $10, $20, $50 and $100) are used for most everyday purposes.

Election time

The president and vice-president are elected every four years. The Senate has two members from each state. Senators are elected for a six-year term. Every two years elections are held for about one-third of the seats in the Senate. The House of Representatives has 435 members elected every two years. The number elected varies from state to state, according to the population of any particular state.

US territories overseas

The USA has various outlying territories and possessions, some of which are self-governing. They include American Samoa, Guam, the Northern Mariana Islands, Belau (Palau), Puerto Rico and the American Virgin Islands.

Holidays and festivals

Public holidays include New Year's Day, (January 1), Martin Luther King's Birthday (3rd Monday in January), Lincoln's Birthday (February 12), Presidents' Day (3rd Monday in February), Memorial Day (last Monday in May), Independence Day (July 4), Labor Day (1st Monday in September), Columbus Day (2nd Monday in October), Veterans Day (November 11), Thanksgiving Day (4th Thursday in November) and Christmas Day.

Some famous Americans

Pocahontas (c1595-1617), daughter of the Native American chief Powhatan

Eli Whitney (1765-1825) invented the cotton gin, a machine for cleaning cotton

John James Audubon (1785-1851), a wildlife artist

Herman Melville (1819-91), the author of *Moby Dick*, a story about the days of whaling

Emily Dickinson (1830-66), one of America's greatest poets

Sitting Bull (c1831-90), a leader of Native American resistance

Mark Twain (1835-1910) wrote *Tom Sawyer* and *Huckleberry Finn*

Thomas Alva Edison (1847-1931) invented the light bulb and the record player

Amelia Earhart (1897-1937), a flying pioneer who disappeared on a round-the-world flight

Ernest Hemingway (1899-1961), a writer of novels and stories

Louis Armstrong (1900-71), a pioneer of jazz

Walt Disney (1901-66), a film animator

Charles Lindbergh (1902-74), the first to fly across the Atlantic Ocean

Jesse Owens (1913-80), track-and-field athlete, star of the 1936 Olympics

Marilyn Monroe (1926-62), a glamorous film actress

Toni Morrison (1931 -), first African-American woman to win the Nobel Prize for literature

Muhammad Ali (1942 -), a world boxing champion

Some key events in history

1513: the Spanish explore Florida

1607: English colony established at Jamestown, Virginia

1625: Dutch colonists found New Amsterdam, later New York City

1773: 'Boston Tea Party' – colonists protest against British rule by dumping tea from British ships into Boston Harbour

1775-1781: American War of Independence

1776 (July 4): Declaration of Independence is signed

1787: US Constitution written

1791: Bill of Rights goes into effect

1803: the Louisiana Purchase from France doubles the size of the USA

1825: opening of the Erie Canal

1838: the first telegraph message, sent by Samuel Morse

1861-1865: the American Civil War

1863: Proclamation to abolish slavery in the USA signed

1869: railway link across the continent completed

1890: the end of the Indian Wars

1917: United States enters the First World War

1929: Stock market crashes, the depression begins

1941: Pearl Harbor bombed; USA enters the Second World War

1945: USA drops atomic bombs on Japan, ending the Second World War

1963: assassination of President John F. Kennedy

1969: Neil Armstrong becomes the first astronaut to land on the Moon

1973: the end of the Vietnam War

Index